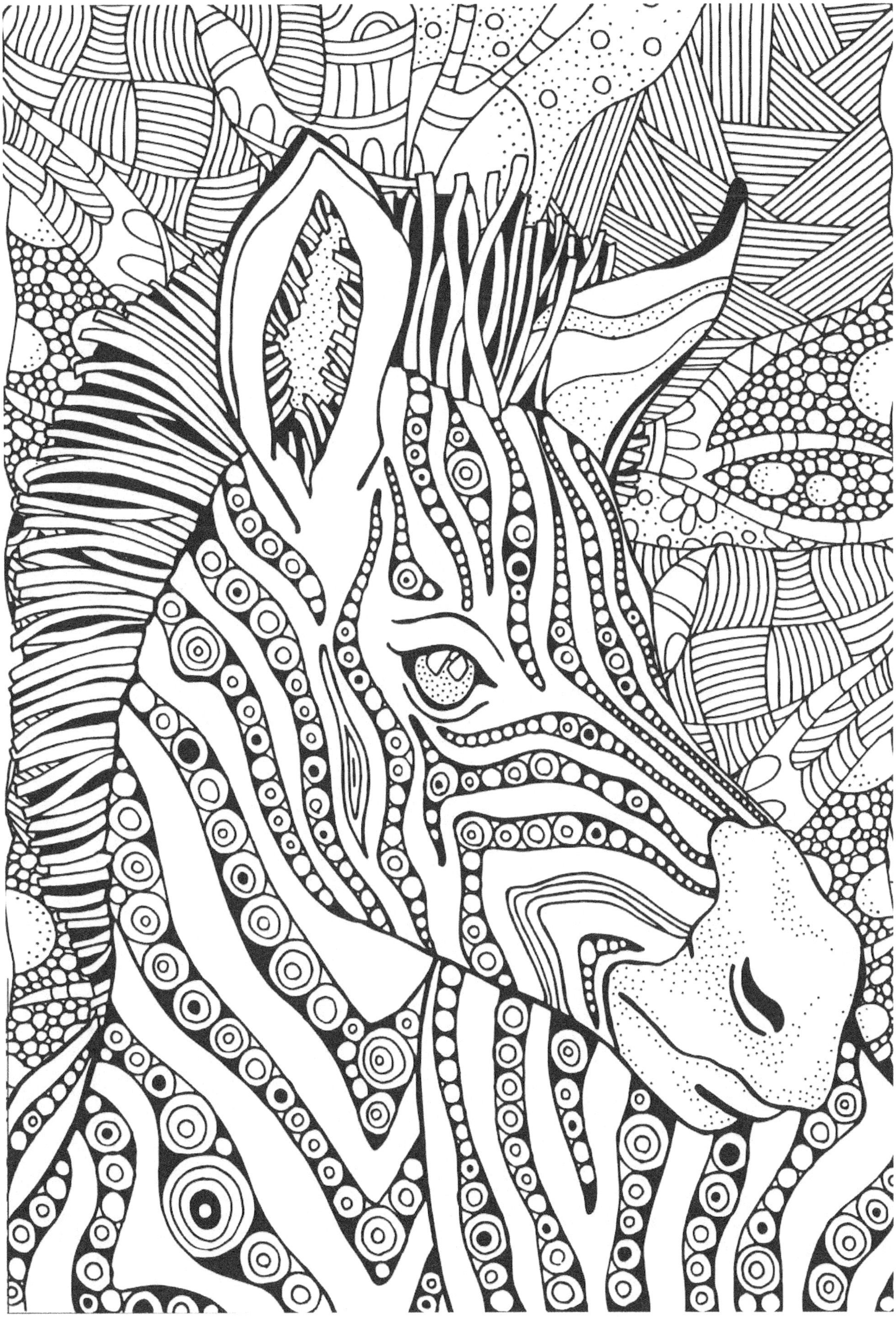

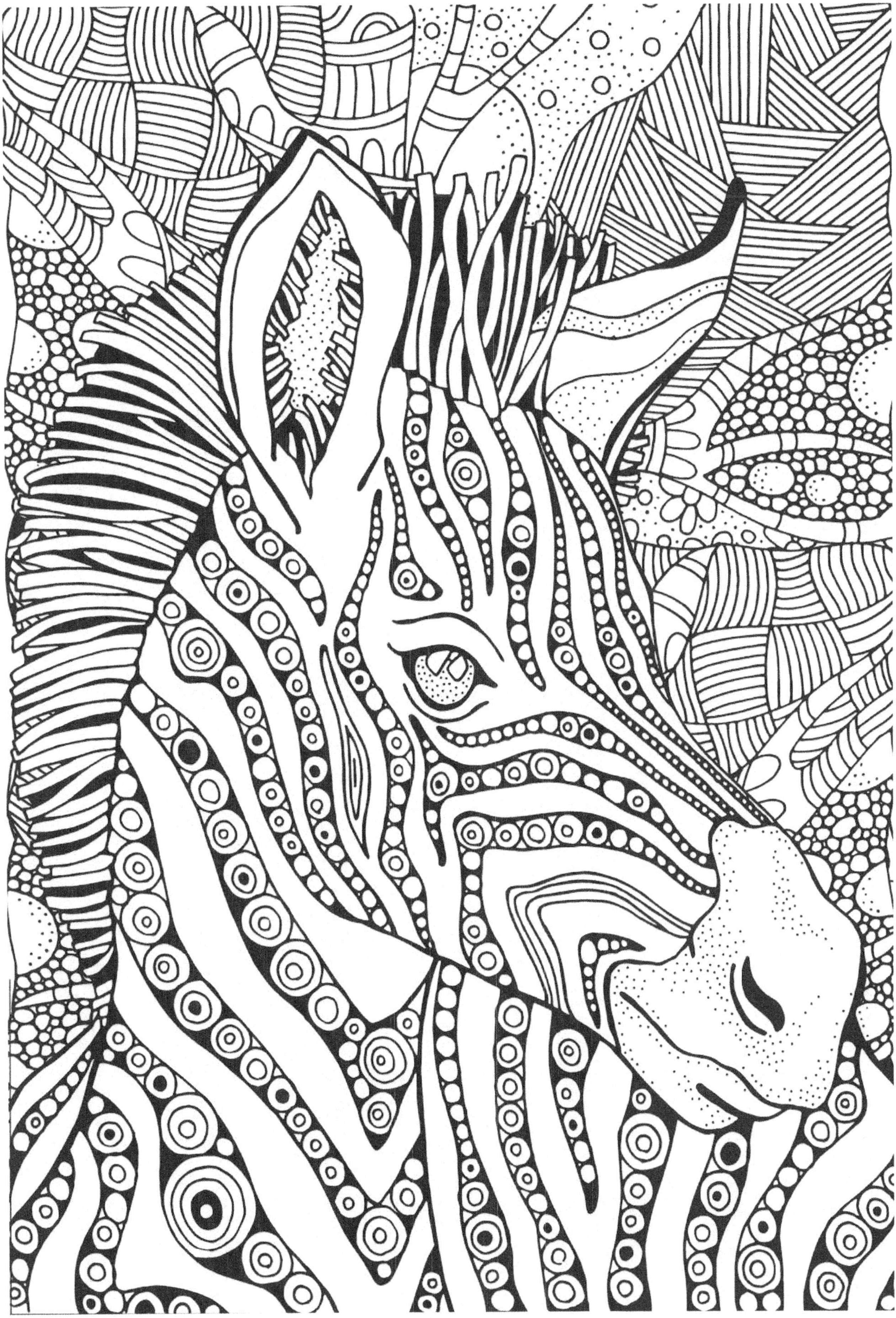

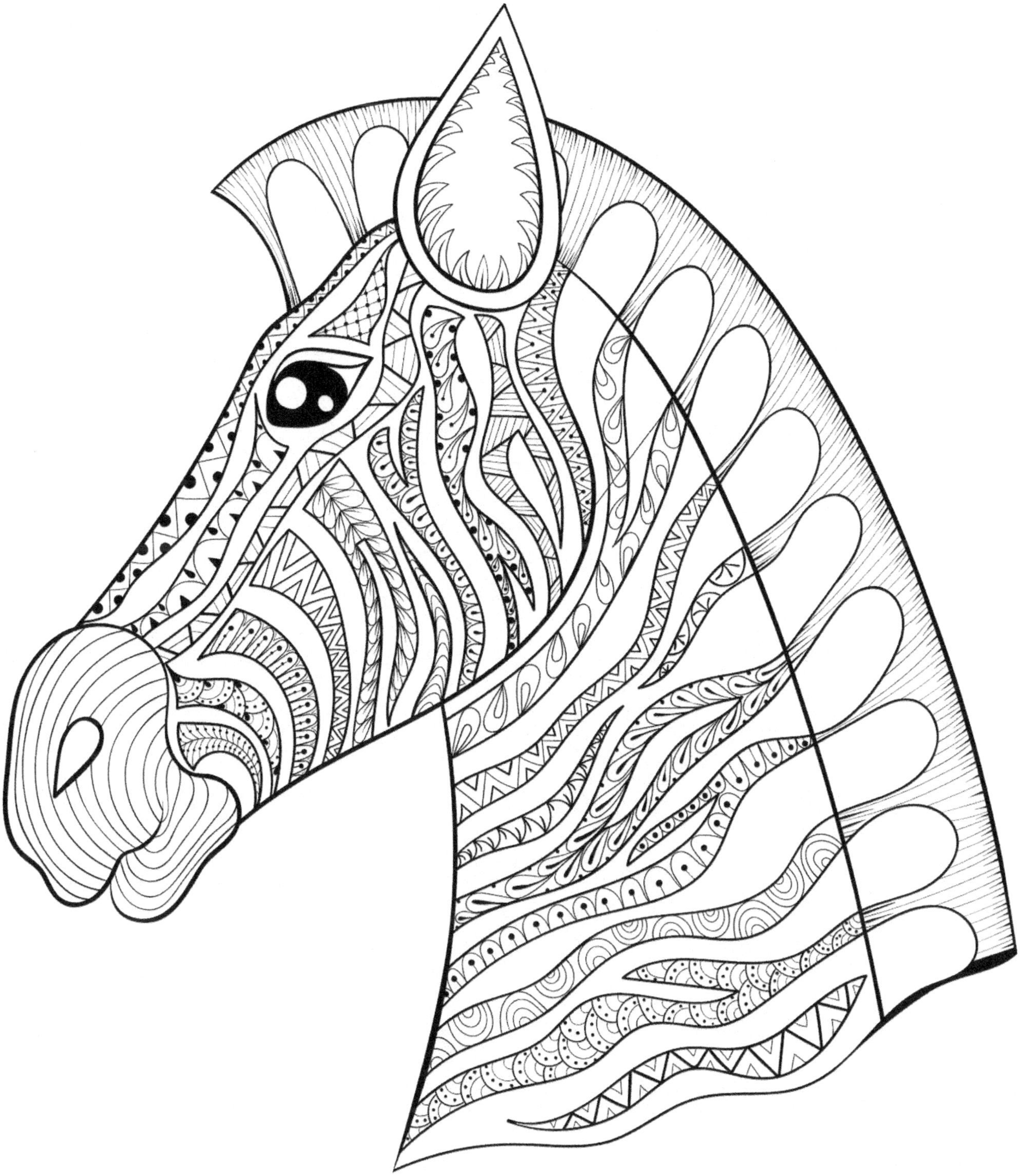

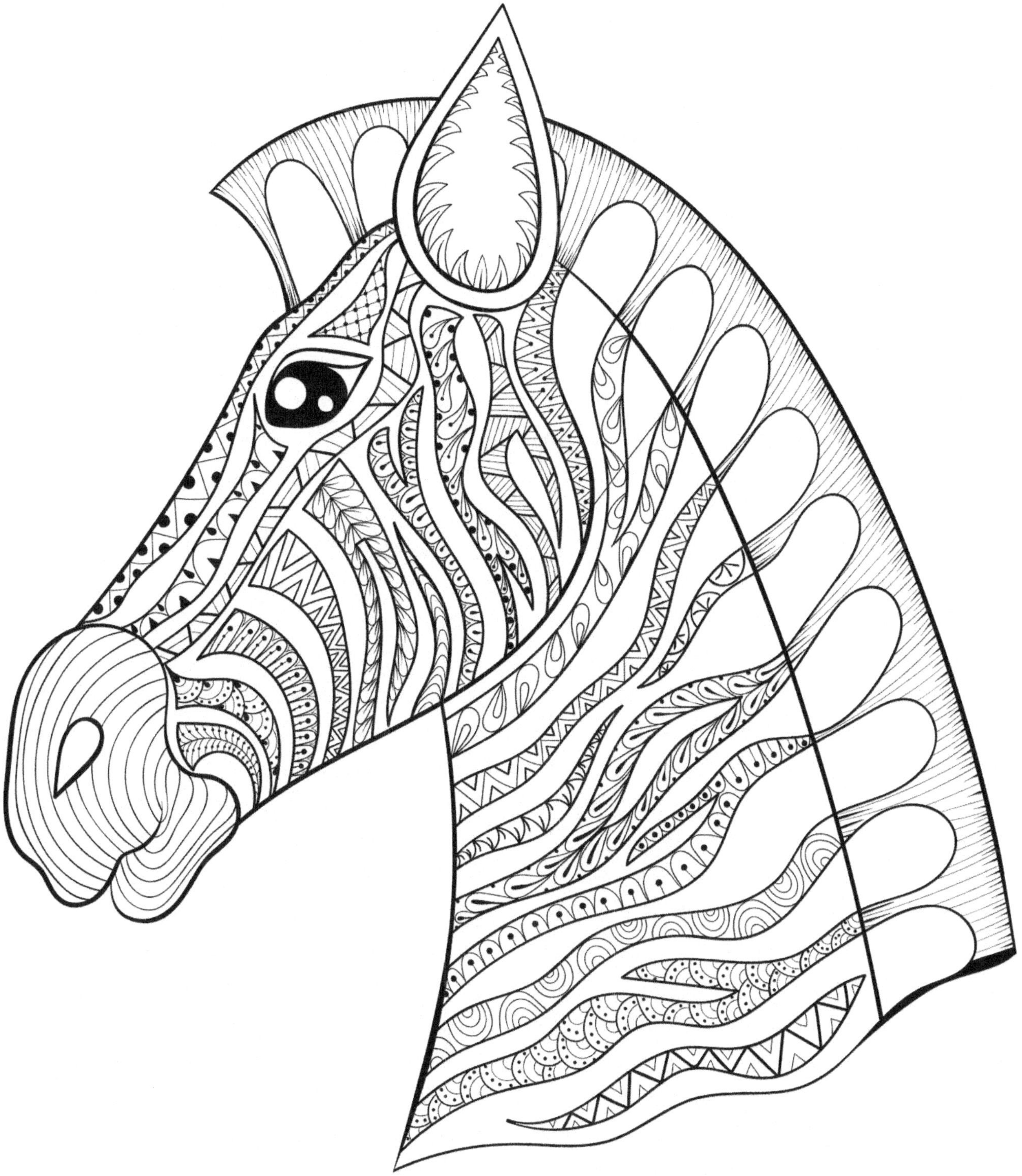

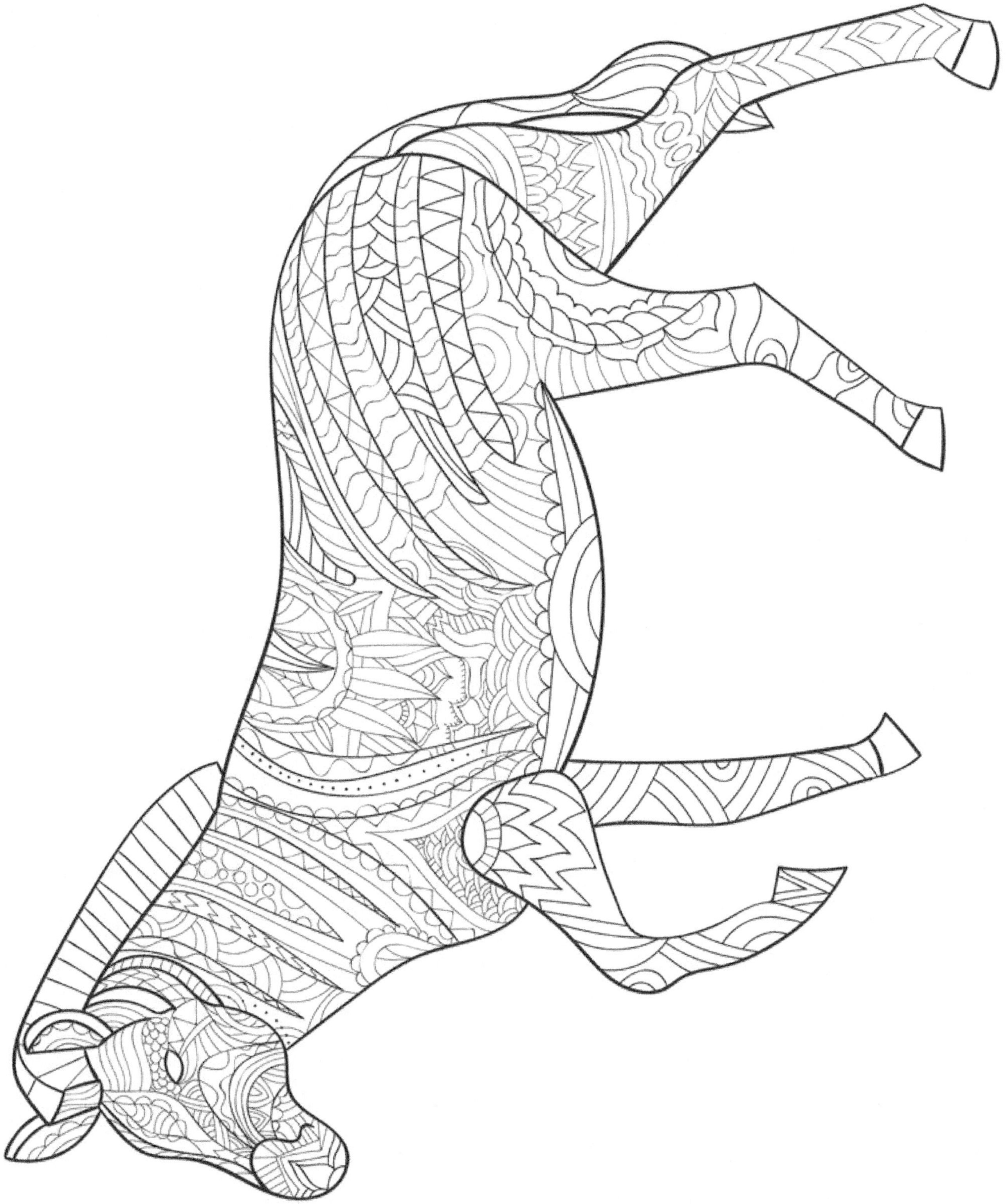

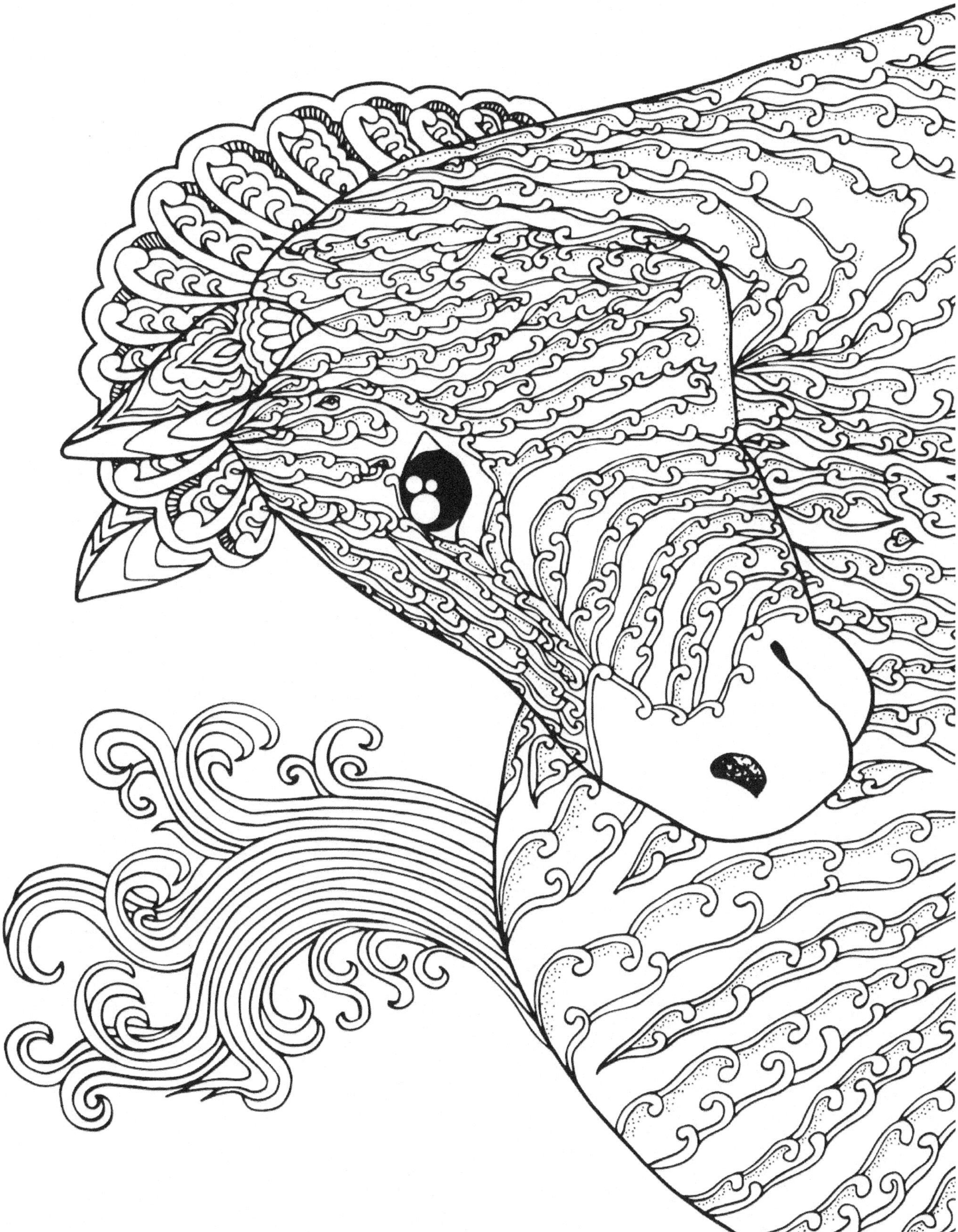

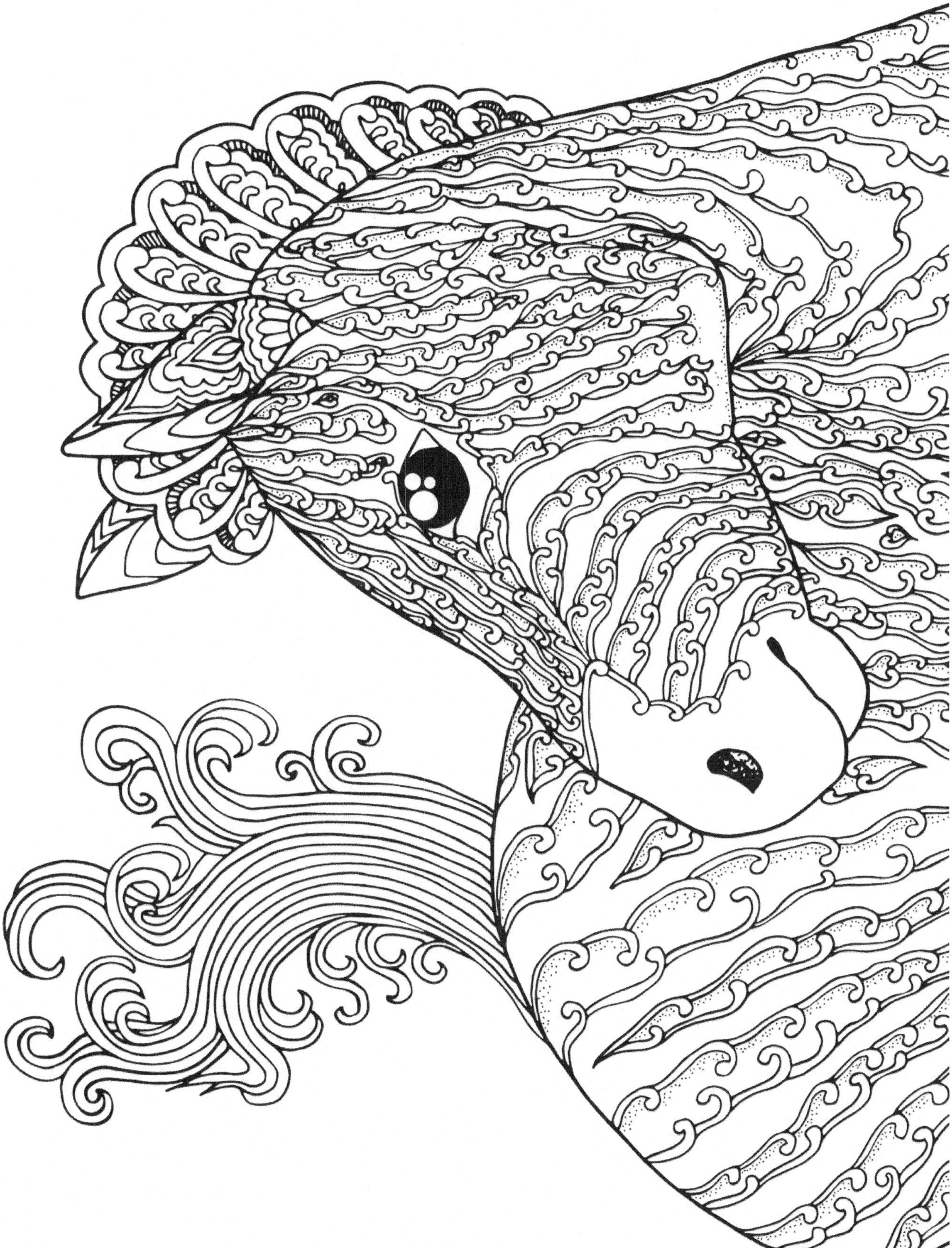

Made in the USA
Las Vegas, NV
01 May 2021

22346236R00046